# MY POETIC MUSINGS
## From a Life of Christian Ministry

By Norman H Drummond

Copyright © 2025 by **Norman H. Drummond**

All rights reserved. No part of this publication may be reproduced, distributed or transmitted in any form or by any means, without prior written permission.

Unless otherwise indicated, Scripture quotations are from the 1999 Updated New Edition American Standard Bible by Zondervan. Used by permission.

**MY POETIC MUSINGS: From a Life of Christian Ministry**

ISBN: 979-8-218-83939-0

# CONTENTS

INTRODUCTION
CHAPTER ONE
    **THE CALL TO CHRISTIAN MINISTRY** ...............................**9**
CHAPTER TWO
    **THE MINISTER'S WORK**.......................................................**17**
CHAPTER THREE
    **CHURCH** ......................................................................................**27**
CHAPTER FOUR
    **PREACHING AND TEACHING** ........................................**37**
CHAPTER FIVE
    **PRAYER**........................................................................................**46**
CHAPTER SIX
    **THE GOSPEL OF JESUS CHRIST**........................................**54**
CHAPTER SEVEN
    **BIBLE STORIES** .......................................................................**63**
CHAPTER EIGHT
    **LOVING PEOPLE**....................................................................**71**
CHAPTER NINE
    **HEAVEN** .....................................................................................**80**
CHAPTER TEN
    **THE CHRISTIAN MINISTER'S FAMILY**............................**89**
FINAL WORDS .......................................................................................100
SCRIPTURE INDEX ..................................................................................102
ABOUT THE AUTHOR.............................................................................107

# INTRODUCTION

"I passed by the field of the sluggard and by the vineyard of the man lacking sense, and behold, it was completely overgrown with thistles; Its surface was covered with nettles, and its stone wall was broken down. When I saw, I reflected upon it; I looked, and received instruction." Proverbs 24:30-32

☙❧

I have observed many things in life that I could not see nor could understand what I was seeing. Saying the ridiculous may give opportunity to ponder in a new direction. Thinking deeply may place you in shallow water, while spending time in the shallows may help you discover more about the sea than drowning ever could.

If you understand any of the above paragraph or the Scripture, it is because you chose to find some meaning even though there might not be any. Writing poetry is for me an exercise in allowing my feelings and thoughts to run free. You may read some of the so-called poetry in this book and find nothing but thistles and nettles. My hope is that the reader who takes time to slowly read will identify with some of the feelings and thoughts or may uncover some of their own. I hope, also, that readers will find themselves attempting to express their own experiences, challenges, and pain through poetry.

Some poetry doesn't rhyme. Some non-rhyming poetry is considered much more creative, artistic, and cerebral than my poetic musings. It is my contention that searching for words to rhyme, while maintaining a beat, and inserting some salient alliteration is fun and often sends my thoughts in different and unexpected directions. You may discover you are a poet and didn't know it.

The sub-title of this book is important. All of these poems are written by me from my experiences in Christian ministry. I am not sure where the phrase originated, but my brother-in-law, Don Wilhite, often repeated from the pulpit this kingdom phrase: "Every Christian is a minister, and every minister has a ministry." I believe this and expect that every active Christian will identify with the ministry experiences that prompted my musing.

This contention that all Christians are ministers is echoed in 2 Corinthians 5:17-18 "Therefore if anyone is in Christ, he is a new creature; and the old things passed away; behold, new things have come. Now all these things are from God, who reconciled the world to Himself through Christ and gave us the ministry of reconciliation, ..." Paul added in verse 20: "Therefore, we are ambassadors for Christ."

Christians often think ministry is only preaching and teaching and when referring to the minister, they are speaking only of the Pastor. It is interesting to note the many types of ministries we observe in the life of Jesus. He was certainly preacher and teacher (Mark 1:15). We are amazed by His healing ministry (Matthew 4:3). He modeled for us a discipling ministry (Matthew 20:17-19). There are various stories depicting His counseling ministry (John 4:16-18). And, He had a children's ministry (Matthew19:13-15). There are other ministries we could identify in Jesus' life. We can, I believe, consider any work we do in the name Jesus Christ, for Gospel of Jesus Christ, and for the church of Jesus Christ, is Christian ministry.

I contend that every Christian should look at whatever their profession is as ministry: Doctors, lawyers, school teachers, sanitation workers, lawn care professionals, social workers, IT specialists, etc. Here is Christian ministry. "Whatever you do in word ore deed, do all in the name of the Lord Jesus, giving thanks through Him to God the Father" (Colossians 3:17).

God has blessed me with many ministry experiences spanning more than 50 years. I began with youth ministry while in college and seminary, was allowed to serve as a pastor for three wonderful but very different churches, enjoyed full-time chaplaincy in a rescue mission, was an active-duty Navy Chaplain serving with Sailors and Marines, and had a few years as Chaplain for senior-adults in an assisted-living community. My prayer is that I used those opportunities to make a difference in the lives of some of those people and positively impacted the Kingdom of God.

Writing poetry has been enjoyable and therapeutic while also a mental and spiritual exercise. Starting from scratch, with a simple thought sparked by some happening or question, soon produces a semi-finished product I can enjoy and share. I say semi-finished because I have learned that if I let time pass after I think I'm finished and pick it up again weeks or months or years later, I hear it differently and see changes that are needed to make it all better. The goal is to end with a satisfying and meaningful finish.

All poems in this book were written by me with two exceptions. In the last chapter of this book are poems about my family. I debated about whether I should include this chapter because these are very personal. One of them was written by my daughter. One of the poems in chapter one on the minister's call was written by my grandmother. My hope is that the chapter on the minister's family will prompt others in ministry to write their own personal poems about family, finding in the process the value of this exercise. I believe your family will love you for it.

My poetic musings have often been used by me as sermon illustrations. They also become a source of reflection on my ministry. As I now put some of them together for a book, I hope they can produce thoughtfulness, become sermon illustrations for preachers and teachers, and encourage ministers to poetic musings of their own. All Scripture passages in this book are from the 1999 Updated New Edition American Standard Bible by the Zondervan Corporation.

No part or poem of this book was written by AI.

I have included a list of Scripture references at the end of this book to assist the reader who may be looking for a possible illustration or for personal reflection of that verse. I have always appreciated authors who have given a Scripture index in their books. You're welcome.

CHAPTER ONE

# THE CALL TO CHRISTIAN MINISTRY

"Therefore I, the prisoner of the Lord, implore you to walk in a manner worthy of the calling with which you have been called, with humility and gentleness with patience, showing tolerance for one another in love, being diligent to preserve the unity of the Spirit in the bond of peace. There is one body and one Spirit, just as also you were called in one hope of your calling." Ephesians 4:1-4

☙❧

I love the label Paul chooses to describe his service to God: "the prisoner of the Lord." I realize that Paul was literally a prisoner at the time of this writing to the church at Ephesus and when he uses the same phrase upon writing to Philemon. However, he sees himself as more than a prisoner of Rome. He is a prisoner of Jesus Christ. That was his chosen identity.

God's calling captivated him. When I was a young man and believed God was calling me into Christian ministry, I asked my pastor for advice. He told me, "If you can do anything else other than ministry, do it." I understood what he meant. If God truly calls you into ministry, you will not be satisfied doing anything else.

Paul's heart and life were endlessly linked to God's calling. He may have been literally in a dark and dingy prison cell, but that condition only reminded him of his other favorite title, "Paul, a bond-servant of

Christ Jesus, called as an apostle, set apart for the gospel of God" (Romans 1:1).

Through my years in ministry, it was God's calling that kept me going; not kind words, not sweet co-workers, not progress, not achievements, and not my determined spirit. When people are mean, when no one appreciates me, when disaster strikes, and when I am tired and weary, it is God's calling, and His continued confirmation of it, that prevents me from quitting.

When Paul writes to Philemon, he describes himself not only as a Prisoner of Jesus Christ, but also in verse nine as "Paul the aged." Some Bible versions translate this "Paul the old man." I cannot compare my life and ministry to the amazing ministry of Paul. I do, however, at this time in my life, see myself in a similar way: called to ministry, a servant of almighty God and His Son Jesus Christ, and an old man.

1. Daniel 6:23 "So Daniel was taken up out of the den and no injury whatever was found on him, because he had trusted in his God."

**STAND FOR GOD**

I will boldly stand for God,
Matters not to me the end,
Whether people call be odd,
Or they throw me in a lion's den.

I will resolutely stand,
Matters not who may oppose,
God is able to demand
Even hungry lion's mouths to close.

Even if I stand alone,
In some dark and dingy cell,
From my mouth shall come no groan,
Even there my God makes all things well.

2. Genesis 12:1,4 "Now the Lord said to Abram, 'Go forth from your country, and from your relatives and from your father's house, to the land which I will show you;"… "So Abram went forth as the Lord had spoken to him…"

## I MUST WHEN GOD LEADS ME

I must when God leads me,
Wherever He needs me,
If modern, remote or unmapped;
At any location,
In any situation,
In spite of conditions, adapt!

I cannot be choosey,
I want God to use me,
I'll readily move if I must.
And, I have decided,
I'll not be indicted
For failing attempts to adjust.

I'm up and proceeding,
Wherever He's leading,
Without any grief or chagrin.
The Lord is my light
And, His way always right
The end of my prayer is: Amen!

3. 2 Corinthians 6:3-5,9-10 "... giving no cause for offense in anything, so that the ministry will not be discredited, but in everything commending ourselves as servants of God, in much endurance, in afflictions, in hardships, in distresses, ... as punished yet not put to death, as sorrowful yet always rejoicing, as poor yet making many rich, as having nothing yet possessing all things."

## THE RIGHT QUESTIONS

The question is not - do I like my assignment?
But, is God's and my will in proper alignment?

Not - will all the family like that we're leaving?
But - is this a signal from God I'm receiving?

Not - can I survive with a salary smaller?
But - is there a call, and is my God the caller?

The question is not - why should I have to do it?
But - is my life's course going just as God drew it?

I've found in the middle of many suggestions,
A servant of God must ask the right questions.

4. Philippians 1:23-24 "But I am hard-pressed from both directions, having the desire to depart and be with Christ, for that is very much better; yet to remain on in the flesh is more necessary for your sake.

## I CANNOT LEAVE, I LOVE THEM

Sometimes I think of changing jobs,
  of doing something better.
I shouldn't have to spend my days

where my best efforts reap no praise.
I could be somewhere less depressing
   spending all my evenings resting.
But, as I start to say, "adieu"
   someone says, "I love you."

I'd like to find some lonely hill
   where I could be a hermit,
Where criticisms can't be heard,
   nor any sick, contrary word,
My self-esteem can there survive,
   and new ideas can grow and thrive,
But just as I'm prepared to quit
   some friend stops by to visit.

I've almost left them many times,
   but could not, would not do it.
In spite of stubbornness and doubt,
   and those who like to whine and pout,
Amid apparent unconcern,
   and knowing not which way to turn.
Although the future looks quite grim,
   I cannot leave. I love them.

5. Hebrews 6:9-12 "But, beloved, we are convinced of better things concerning you, and things that accompany salvation, though we are speaking in this way. For God is not unjust so as to forget your work and the love which you have shown toward His name, in having ministered and in still ministering to the saints. And we desire that each one of you show the same diligence so as to realize the full assurance of hope until the end,"

## I WILL NOT RESIGN

Could God provide another place,
Where people really love their pastor?
Desiring a quicker pace,
And not afraid of growing faster?
Yet until God has changed my mind, I'll not resign.

It's true a few have no respect.
They don't appreciate my toil.
Harsh words have had an ill effect.
On seeing certain ones I coil!
And, yet God hasn't sent a sign, I'll not resign.

Though skies of blue turn darkest grey,
My laboring will not diminish.
God led me here and here I'll stay,
Continuing until I finish.
Then God will let me know it's time, and I'll resign.

6. Judges 6:36-38 "Then Gideon said to God, 'If You will deliver Israel through me, as You have spoken, behold, I will put a fleece of wool on the threshing floor. If there is dew on the fleece only, and it is dry on all the ground, then I will know that You will deliver Israel through me, as You have spoken.'"

## GIVE ME A SIGN

Dear Jesus, I love you.
    Serving you is a joy,
An honor and privilege
    Your plans to employ.
I don't want to change things.

I don't mean to whine,
But Lord, it would help me if you gave me a sign.

Each step of my journey
    I'm walking by faith.
I trust in Your word, Lord,
        And all that Thou saith.
But sometimes I wonder
    if our ways align.
It would help me a little, if you gave me a sign.

I notice on Sunday
    the pews are not filled.
I'm praying that one day
    our ardor will build.
Has my life lost passion?
    Am I failing to shine?
I really, really need You to give me a sign.

A lady approached me
    as church was dismissed.
She has many troubles,
    many woes that persist.
Today she just wanted
    to credit the Divine,
For sending me there. Lord! Was that my sign?

7. Acts 21:5 "When our days there were ended, we left and started on our journey, while they all, with wives and children, escorted us until we were out of the city. After kneeling down on the beach and praying, we said farewell to one another."

## LEAVING ONE CHURCH FOR ANOTHER

Emotions of sadness and joy are growing,
My heart and my eyes very near overflowing.
The mixture of feeling's immense upon knowing,
The sorrow of leaving and pleasure in going.

My thoughts are of children, of fathers and mothers.
The people I leave and my new Christian brothers,
Extremes of emotion each pastor discovers,
In forsaking some for a call to help others.

The tension that leaving and going's creating
Has little effect on the fact I am stating.
Though sadly I leave there is no altercating.
I must leave my home for a home God has waiting.

CHAPTER TWO

# THE MINISTER'S WORK

Acts 20:18-21 "You yourselves know, from the first day that I set foot in Asia, how I was with you the whole time, serving the Lord with all humility and with tears and with trials which came upon me through the plots of the Jews; how I did not shrink from declaring to you anything that was profitable, and teaching you publicly and from house to house, solemnly testifying to both Jews and Greeks of repentance toward God and faith in our Lord Jesus Christ."

❧❦

If you have been serving the Lord in some full-time or part-time ministry, you will probably not be surprised to hear me say that most of the people to whom you minister have no idea how much work is involved in doing ministry. They are only aware of the time you appear before them to teach, or preach, or lead some activity. It may not help much for you to try to explain it to them. They cannot identify with what you do.

It is sort of funny to hear Paul trying to explain his work to his people. "You yourselves know, from the first day that I set foot in Asia, how I was with you the whole time, serving the Lord …" I suppose they understood on some level. Read his whole speech in Acts chapter twenty. He warns that opposition to his ministry will attempt to "speak perverse things" to draw them away from his work and teachings. Defending his ministry Paul tells them to remember, "that night and day for a period of three years I did not cease to admonish each one with tears."

There are many anxious, worry-filled, and tearful times in Christian ministry. There are also many thrilling, fruitful, satisfying, and joyful moments. It is helpful to keep in mind the saying sometimes attributed to President Harry Truman: "It's amazing what you can accomplish if you don't care who gets the credit." And don't forget Ephesians 3:20-21: "to Him who is able to do far more abundantly beyond all that we ask or think, according to the power that is within us, to Him be the glory in the church and in Christ Jesus to all generations forever and ever. Amen"

I have often prayed, after leaving a place of ministry to go to another, "Oh Lord, I pray that something I did or said made a difference in someone's life, and that Your work will continue in them." Maybe one day we will know. Until then …

1. 2 Timothy 2:8-10 "Remember Jesus Christ, risen from the dead, descendant of David, according to my gospel, for which I suffer hardship even to imprisonment as a criminal; but the word of God is not imprisoned. For this reason I endure all things for the sake of those who are chosen, so that they also may obtain the salvation which is in Christ Jesus and with it eternal glory."

## **WORKING FOR GOD**

Sometimes I can get so excited while doing,
That soon I forget who I'm doing it for.
I can get so involved in all things that are brewing,
It often appears that I think I know more,
Than He who has made me and keeps me and gave me
This work which I find so fulfilling and fun.

I guess I think God will be able to save me,
If I should do something I should not have done.

I jump into serving without ever waiting
To hear what my Master has planned for my day,
But now I can see this is wrong, so I'm stating:
"I will not continue to do things that way."
From now on I'll start out each workday by saying:
"I'm working for God and not self anymore."
And, all that I do will be done after praying,
I will not forget who I'm doing it for!

2. Ecclesiastes 3:1-4 "There is an appointed time for everything, and there is a time for every event under heaven – A time to give birth and a time to die; a time to plant and a time to uproot what is planted. A time to kill and a time to heal; a time to tear down and a time to build up, A time to weep and a time to laugh; a time to mourn and a time to dance."

## WORK IS NEVER DONE

Never stop and never rest.
Always go and give your best.
Never slow and never faint.
Stay on top for you're a saint!

Keep it up and move along.
Preach and pray and sing a song.
Every day without a break,
Spill your cup for Jesus' sake!

All the great men gave their all.
Never sit but stand up tall.

You can't quit, no not right now.
Delegate? I don't know how!

Dear sweet wife is safe at home.
Doesn't mind these nights alone.
She's the kind who understands,
Preacher's life means much demands!

Heart attacks and belly aches,
Haunt the small and not the greats.
People call, don't let them wait.
Don't relax or meditate!

Out of breath? Still run your race.
Question not the glorious pace,
Tis your lot (Though some would deem,
Our early death the devil's dream).

3. Psalm 91:10-11 "No evil will befall you, nor will any plague come near your tent. For He will give His angels charge concerning you, to guard you in all your ways."

## WHEN TROUBLE HOVERS

When trouble hovers over us
    and wants our life destroyed.
When wickedness surrounding us
    has picked and tricked and toyed;
God's love has not withdrawn from us,
    his angels are deployed.
Ole Satan can't bring harm to us
    his acts may have annoyed,
But God is holding on to us

        we'll soon be overjoyed,
For powers in this universe
        cannot His power avoid.

4. 2 Timothy 1:6-7 "For this reason I remind you to kindle afresh the gift of God which is in you through the laying on of my hands. For God has not given us a spirit of timidity, but of power and love and discipline."

## IF GOD GAVE ME POWER

If God gave me power to heal,
        When I touch any sick or diseased,
But promised I quickly would lose it,
        If I used it and he was not pleased.
I wonder how long I could last,
        Till I thoughtlessly used my new gift,
As a way of attracting attention,
        Instead of God's Name to uplift.

If God gave me power to predict,
        What the future was going to be,
But explained its purpose to convict,
        And confirm He is working through me.
I wonder how long it would take,
        Till I vainly misused my new gift,
To gain power and fond recognition,
        Instead of His Name to uplift.

My God gave me power in weakness,
        To serve Him with gifts that He chose.
He has given me mildness and meekness,
        His blessing eternally flows.

I wonder how Long it will be,
    Till I fully make use of His gift,
To serve Him with complete devotion,
    And always His Name to uplift.

5. 1 John 5:4-5 "For whatever is born of God overcomes the world; and this is the victory that has overcome the world – our faith. Who is the one who overcomes the world, but he who believes that Jesus is the Son of God."

## A WINNING ATTITUDE

An attitude of winning
Is difficult beginning,
But once begun begins to build.
I will no longer choose to yield,

I will praise God completely,
To all that would defeat me.
The failures of the past
Will be forgotten fast,

And moving on I'll find
A different state of mind,
A state of deep conviction,
Fervor with no restriction,

And now though just a beginner,
I choose to be God's winner.

6. Philippians 4: 13 "I can do all things through Him who strengthens me."

## TO DO ALL THIS

To humbly walk each day,
In everything to pray,
The Word of God to read,
And all its' council heed,
To keep a good report,
And lovingly exhort.

To turn the other cheek,
To stand beside the weak,
To bind the broken hearted,
To reunite those parted,
To patiently equip,
And tame my tongue and lip.

To douse the devil's darts,
To soften hardened hearts,
To stand and without shame,
The truth of God proclaim,
In criticisms face,
Continuing the pace.

To feed the hungry sheep,
To climb the mountain steep,
To make each foe a friend,
To fight unto the end,
To be a shining light,
And turn from wrong to right.

To do all this I know
Impossible, although,
A possibility

Through Christ who strengthens me.

7. Matthew 11:29-30 "Take My yoke upon you and learn from Me, for I am gentle and humble in heart, and you will find rest for your souls, for My yoke is easy and My burden is light."

## **BEING PASTOR IS HARD?**

I have heard ministers say,
    "Being pastor is hard."
        I'm suspicious of this estimation.
Were they expecting to play,
    While just loving the Lord,
        Or expecting some blessed recreation?

Do most of our days
    Include labor and work,
        Like construction, firefighter, or battle master?
Are most members amazed
    Or puzzled or irked
        By a claim of hard work by the pastor?

Being pastor is dizzy
    With counseling and caring,
        Needing patience and grace and regard.
The position is busy
    With studies and preparing,
        All fulfilling but not very hard.

Don't misread my intention
    As devaluation,
        Of a pastor's position and charter.
I musingly mention

The minister in question,
>should not imply our work is much harder.

8. Proverbs 4:5-8 "Acquire wisdom! Acquire understanding! Do not forget nor turn away from the words of my mouth. Do not forsake her, and she will guard you; love her, and she will watch over you, the beginning of wisdom is: Acquire wisdom; and with all your acquiring, get understanding. Prize her, and she will exalt you; she will honor you if you embrace her."

## MY LIBRARY

My library needs a makeover.
Personal books collected,
More than fifty years gathering dust,
Racked on cluttered, bowing shelves,
Holding various other artifacts.

Books with yellowed covers.
Others looking fresh and new,
Never myself thumbed through,
While others broken, bent and bruised,
Looking tired upon the shelf.

Upright stacked together.
Different colors, different fonts,
No topical directory, none,
Paperback or hard, jutting, slumping,
Holding tightly their stories.

Rows and rows of volumes.
Wrappers stare at me disgusted,
That I leave them sitting there,

Disheveled, neglected, wasting,
Unappreciated paper.

CHAPTER THREE

# CHURCH

Acts 14:22-23 "… strengthening the souls of the disciples, encouraging them to continue in the faith, and saying, 'Through many tribulations we must enter the kingdom of God.' When they had appointed elders for them in every church, having prayed with fasting, they commended them to the Lord in whom they had believed."

☙❧

The local church is a fragile thing. Of course I am speaking about the local congregation of believers; not the ever, cash sucking structures with dedicated parts and other parts decaying, whose walls, the color of which, once broke apart the fellowship, and decisions to change anything about the buildings is greeted with, "But it has always been like this." You know what I mean! The buildings are not the church, but the buildings are often the center of the church's attention and a big source of the church's problems.

The people who inhabit the buildings (though mostly only on Sunday) are the local body of Christ, commissioned to take the gospel message to the world and to make disciples. I'm not sure why the church is so fragile, but I know that it is. Paul illustrated this fragility as he described how each individual part of the body grumbles against the other. "And the eye cannot say to the hand 'I have no need of you"; or again the head to the feet, 'I have no need of you" (1 Corinthians 12:21).

There are a few things you can do to reveal how delicate and fragmentable your church is. Move or remove one piece of furniture from the worship platform without asking. Or, suggest a small change in the order of worship. Or, fail to recognize which member in the church holds the power of the purse or which member is the true matriarch. Just push the right button or touch the wrong nerve.

However, some within each local body of believers have received a call to Christian ministry. Some who have received a ministry call are actively, in Christ Jesus, holding the body together.

They function in their individual ministry to accomplish the work Luke describes in this chapter's opening verse. "Encouraging them to continue in the faith, and saying, 'Through many tribulations we must enter the kingdom of God.'" Though the local body of believers can be difficult, we love her as does our Lord Jesus. "… Christ also loved the church and gave Himself up for her…" (Ephesians 5:25).

And so, we have as our task, the same as Paul's message to the elders of the church at Ephesus: "Be on guard for yourselves and for all the flock, among which the Holy Spirit has made you overseers, to shepherd the church of God which He purchased with His own blood" (Acts 20:28).

1. Psalm 37:4-7 "Delight yourself in the Lord; and He will give you the desires of your heart. Commit your way to the Lord, trust also in Him, and He will do it. He will bring forth your righteousness as the light and your judgement as the noonday. Rest in the Lord and wait patiently for Him;"

## MY HEART'S DESIRE (Not what you might think)

In Psalm thirty-seven verse four,
We are promised desires of our heart,
If we delight ourselves in the Lord.
And as I on each mission embark,
One such desire I implore,
For a Luke or a Silas or Mark.

Paul's fellow workers assisted.
In labors they lifted his load.
Whenever some people resisted,
They stood and were faithful and bold,
And I also wish there existed,
Helpers in church of that mold.

Pastors need some special persons,
"God sent" to help me to stand.
Like Silas was with Paul's excursions.
In suffering or struggles at hand.
I thank God, in my ministry were some,
Like AJ, Ed, Larry and Dan.

So, wherever you send me to serve,
Here is the desire of my heart Lord:
A person to watch my back,
A person to keep me straight,
A person with skills that I lack,
A person to take things off my plate,
A person to share in my vision,
A partner in faith and in prayer,
A person to join me in mission,
A person with patience to spare.

2. 1 Thessalonians 2:10-11 "You are witnesses, and so is God, how devoutly and uprightly and blamelessly we behaved toward you believers; just as you know how we were exhorting and encouraging and imploring each one of you as a father would his own children."

## THE PERSONALITY OF A CHURCH

When ministers stay for very long
    within a churches' favor,
Invariably the church adopts
    the minister's behavior.
If comical and full of fun
    their minister should be,
Eventually the church develops
    as humorous a sense as he.
Whenever a minister proves to hold
    a mighty faith in God,
You'll find a people who are bold,
    and never need a prod.
So, whether kind or musical,
    or socially concerned,
The church's personality
    will gradually be turned,
Assuming little qualities
    their minister displays,
The church's character is formed:
    its grace, its wit, its ways.
This means that ministers must be
    sure their personal behaviors,
Are well controlled and clearly based
    on traits that are our Savior's
And anytime we criticize
    a church's quality,

Remember, they just imitate
>	the character they see.

3. Psalm 34:18 "The Lord is near to the brokenhearted and saves those who are crushed in spirit."

**RELIEVE THEIR PAIN**

It is difficult, I know,
For this whole church to trust me.
They have seen pastors come and go,
While they remain to reap results of foolish plans.

Decisions come slow.
They first must get to know me.
Still wincing from a bruising blow,
For now, just out of caution, they will bind my hands.

Letting wounds heal.
I hope they soon believe me.
Love was the last pastor's appeal,
Their faith and love will not be won so soon again.

Every day I kneel,
I pray, "Dear Lord, live though me!
Lead these sweet people in Your will.
Through honest, open, loving paths relieve their pain."

4. 2 Corinthians 9:6-7 "Now this I say, he who sows sparingly will also reap sparingly and he who sows bountifully will also reap bountifully. Each one must do just as he has purposed in his heart, not grudgingly or under compulsion, for God loves a cheerful giver."

## GIVE (to your church)

Give as you would if an angel
Awaited your gift at the door.
Give as you would if tomorrow
Depended on giving some more.

Give as you would if a gun
Was held to your head by a crook.
Give as you would if a huge muscular man
Turned you upside down and shook.

Give as you would if you gave
From the wallet of someone next to you.
Give as you would if you knew
If not giving this church could sue you.

Give as you would if some creature
Needed money so it would not eat you.
Give as you would if by giving
Your wife would not evilly treat you.

Give as you would just to stop
This poem from making you tearful.
But always remember when giving
Give from a heart that is cheerful.

5. Acts 27:34-37 "'Therefore I encourage you to take some food, for this is for your preservation, for not a hair from the head of any of you will perish.' Having said this, he took bread and gave thanks to God in the presence of all, and he broke it and began to eat. All of them were encouraged and they themselves also took food. All of us in the ship were two hundred and seventy-six persons."

## ABOARD A MIGHTY SHIP AT SEA

Aboard a mighty ship at sea
  Are no majestic shrines,
    Stained glass designs,
      Soft cushions for the knee,
  Just troubled minds.

There are no lofty choirs heard,
  Or polished organ keyed,
    No brass or reed,
      Just now and then a bird,
  And men in need.

There is no lovely chapel yard
  Upon the rolling wave,
    No hedge to shave,
      No grass to grow and guard,
  Just souls to save.

And there on board the men are met
  With open arms that care,
    God's love to share,
      For God has wisely set
  A Chaplain there.

6. Exodus 16:1-2 " … On the fifteenth day of the second month after their departure from the land of Egypt. The whole congregation of the sons of Israel grumbled against Moses and Aaron in the wilderness, …"

## EV'RY BODY KNOWS

Ev'rybody knows precisely
   What the minister ought to do,
      And exactly how they feel he ought to act.
They have figured out in numbers
   What his working should ensue,
      And, informing him does not require tact.

Ev'ry day brings one more chance
   To let the minister know they know,
      That the minister isn't doing all he ought.
And they never mean to indicate
   That they are friend or foe,
      And will tell him, what he thinks they are, they're not.

Ev'ry minister must expect
   To be exposed to gibes and jeers,
      Even as he proves to be their very best.
God will give assurance which
   Does not depend on cheers,
      And, will grant sufficient strength to pass the test.

7. 2 Corinthians 12:7 "Because of the surpassing greatness of the revelations, for this reason, to keep me from exalting myself, there was given me a thorn in the flesh, a messenger of Satan to torment me –to keep me from exalting myself!"

## A GREAT THORN

In my side I have got a great thorn,
An embarrassment from the day I was born.
It's a great big thorn yes,

And I humbly confess:
"I believe my thorn's bigger than yourn."

I, like Paul, have prayed, "Lord remove!"
It's presence I can't even prove.
It's a hindrance at work,
Has me going berserk,
And, I'm certain it's bigger than you've.

The thorn which I rue is no person,
Not infirmity, vice, or perversion.
It's hard to explain,
It gives me no gain.
But I know, of all thorns mine's the worse one.

I can't say that I know what was Paul's.
If was eye problems, speech, or in-laws.
We must only surmise
That of thorns his was prize.
But my thorn is still bigger than all's.

About thorns I don't mean to jest.
There exists in me something I've addressed,
That occasionally appears,
Causing trouble and tears,
Like Paul's thorn, God allows as a quest.

8. 1 Corinthians 12:14 "For the body is not one member, but many. If the foot says, 'Because I am not an eye, I am not a part of the body,' it is not for this reason any the less a part of the body."

## FEET GIVE US PAWS

There aren't many poems about feet.
Poses Redford in a great movie.
Poems on heart, fingers, face,
'Bout hands, legs and all that bass,
But foot rhymes are rare, not replete.

Why would our feet not command
More poet's attention? They're groovy!
A soldier depends on all toes
On their feet when facing fit foes,
So, they give all the care feet demand.

More than one of great Bible passages
Is found with high praises of feet.
Isaiah and Nahum and Paul
Call beautiful are feet to all,
Of those who bear good messages.

Feet are an honorable emblem,
To wash others' feet Christ encouraged.
One woman did that with her tears.
Some leaving the tomb amidst fears
Found Jesus and at His feet loved Him.

Sad was the foot to have pleaded
That if not a hand, not important.
Church members, God bless 'em!
Miss this foot and hand lesson.
Every part of the body is needed!

CHAPTER FOUR

# PREACHING AND TEACHING

"Acts 5:40-42 "... And after calling the apostles in, they flogged them and ordered them not to speak in the name of Jesus, and then released them. So they went on their way from the presence of the Council, rejoicing that they had been considered worthy to suffer shame for His name. And every day, in the temple and from house to house, they kept right on teaching and preaching Jesus as the Christ."

☙❦

It is interesting to me that the act of preaching is very often in Scripture connected with teaching as in the passage above saying the apostles "kept right on teaching and preaching." Two other places in the book of Acts link together teaching and preaching: Acts 15:35 and 28:31. Luke 20:1 records that, "On one of the days while He [Jesus] was teaching the people in the temple and preaching the gospel ..." Paul, writing to Timothy tells him, "The elders who rule well are to be considered worthy of double honor, especially those who work hard at preaching and teaching" (1 Timothy 5:17).

There must be some difference between preaching and teaching. If not, this frequent combination would be a redundancy. Some preachers may consider the difference to be decibels. Preaching is louder than teaching. I think the difference is that preaching involves more persuasion, admonition, and confrontation than teaching. I propose that what is important to note is that both should happen. Standing before our brothers and sisters we should both teach and preach.

I contend that the passage in Ephesians regarding gifts of the Holy Spirit links together "pastors and teachers" as one gift that involves teaching and preaching (Ephesians 4:11). Certainly, the role of pastor/shepherd includes persuasion and admonition. Our Lord, as shepherd, "guides me in the paths of righteousness." His "rod and staff comfort me" (Psalm 23). I have always considered it a compliment when a church member calls me "preacher." The pastor is shepherd and preacher and teacher.

The question is, are Christians who are called into other ministries than pastor/shepherd also to preach and teach? In Acts chapter six through eight we read that two of the men, Stephen and Philip, selected to serve as deacon, taking on the task of assuring that widows had their "daily serving of food" (Acts 6:1), also had a preaching ministry. Neither were pastors. 1 Timothy 5:17 says, "The elders who rule well are to be considered worthy of double honor, especially those who work hard at preaching and teaching." Were all those elders pastors?

Always step carefully through the process of understanding and interpreting what Scripture actually says. How should we understand Titus 2:3-5? "Older women likewise are to be reverent in their behavior, not malicious gossips nor enslaved in much wine, teaching what is good, so that they may encourage the young women to love their husbands, to love their children, to be sensible, pure, workers at home, kind, being subject to their own husbands, so that the word of God will not be dishonored." Teachers? Concerned with the Word of God? Of course!

Paul told Pastor Timothy to pass along to others the task of teaching. "The things which you have heard from me in the presence of many witnesses, entrust these to faithful men who will be able to teach others also (2 Timothy 2:2). Especially for those of you whom God has called into Christian ministry, I expect that you all would find in your ministry opportunities to preach and teach.

1. Mark 1:38 "He [Jesus] said to them, 'Let us go somewhere else to the towns nearby so that I may preach there also; for that is what I came for.'"

### I CAME TO PREACH

Eyes half-closed, ears never opened.
Men who've dozed any time I preach.
Children play, mouths never stopping,
Mothers stay far from children's reach.

Smiles and grins are everywhere,
Caused by someone's messy hair,
Or a child's peculiar stare,
Noisy car or noisy chair,
Seemingly they do not care,
For any truth that I might bear.

Though I bleed, my Bible opened,
I proceed. Out to all I reach.
Even though all are not listening,
I still know, I came to preach.

2. 1 Corinthians 2:4-5 "… and my message and my preaching were not in persuasive words of wisdom, but in demonstration of the Spirit and of power, so that your faith would not rest on the wisdom of men, but on the power of God."

## YOU PREACHED IT VERY WELL

This mornings' message was so good,
You preached it very well,
And I could see from where I stood,
Each head on which it fell.

I liked the extra things you said,
That were not in my notes,
On every single toe you tread,
Of both the sheep and goats.

And as I gave the invitation,
You reached the heart of some,
Who in their sinful situation,
I thought would never come.

Tonight, O Spirit, preach once more
My mouth, my heart control.
A patient, moving message pour,
Into each listening soul.

And when I'm told, "That was so good!"
And for my hand their reaching,
I'll say, "well sir, I only stood,
The Spirit did the preaching."

3. 2 Timothy 3:16-17 "All Scripture is inspired by God and profitable for teaching, for reproof, for correction, for training in righteousness; so that the man of God may be adequate, equipped for every good work."

## GOD INSPIRED

Fresh concepts, thoughts, ideas arise,
As from God's Word I read.
I gather crumbs, God multiplies,
A sermon forms before my eyes,
To meet the masses' need.

I stand amazed before each line,
God given, God inspired.
I cannot call one sermon mine,
I praise the Lord for thoughts divine,
To keep our spirits fired.

Excitement grows as Sunday nears.
This message burns inside.
I pray Dear God, please open ears,
From stoney hearts bring contrite tears,
As man and truth collide.

The sermon done I give the call.
"God, cause them to be brave.
Convict the lost both big and small,
O Holy One convict them all,
To call on Thee to save."

4. 2 Timothy 4:2 "… preach the word; be ready in season and out of season; reprove, rebuke, exhort, with great patience and instruction."

## WHAT WOULD YOU HAVE ME TO SAY?

What would You have me to say today
    to the people I pass on the street?

Should I convey in some simple way
>    how the love that You give is complete?
Should I reveal to the world Your will
>    that all people on earth know your love?
Or, should I impart, it is from Your heart
>    That You sent us Your Son from above?
And, must I explain how Your Son was slain
>    so the price for our sin would be paid?
And, must I disclose how new life comes to those
>    Who believing, receive You today?

All my inquiring is tiring I know
>    when we know that we know what to do.
All of my questions make little impressions
>    on Saints who know ain't nothing new.

We must expound that in Jesus we've found
>    a true Savior who gives to us these:
In life - love and joy, forgiveness and glory
>    and, in death - He gives eternal peace.
All this we can utter and shout and not mutter
>    this message we'll spread far and near.
God's message we'll carry, and with all we'll share Thee
>    All this we will do without fear.
But, Lord as we share, and Your story we bear,
>    Some things of you we want to ask.
Let love be apparent and faith be inherent
>    And, telling be never a task.

5. Psalm 116:5-8 "Yes, our God is compassionate. The Lord preserves the simple; I was brought low, and He saved me. Return to your rest, O my soul, for the Lord has dealt bountifully with you. For you have

rescued my soul from death, my eyes from tears, my feet from stumbling."

## SHE WAS CRYING

She was crying.
Someone pushed her down.
I was trying,
to wipe away her frown.
I explained,
"If you'll just hold my hand,
I'll listen to what happened,
and I'll try to understand."

It didn't matter,
what actually occurred.
She was hurt,
and wanted to be heard.
She explained.
I listened with my heart,
And watched a friendship growing,
as I watched her tears depart.

It was time,
to teach a Bible story.
I stepped out,
with all the kids before me.
I explained.
She listened with her heart.
I told about a place with God,
where pain and tears depart.

6. Isaiah 55:10-11 "For the rain and the snow come down from heaven, and do not return there without watering the earth and making it bear and sprout, and furnishing seed to the sower and bread to the eater; so will My word be which goes forth from My mouth; it will not return to Me empty without accomplishing what I desire, and without succeeding in the matter for which I sent it,"

## THE BOY DIDN'T LISTEN

The boy didn't listen,
he very rarely did.
A handful plus, he really was
a hard to manage kid.

He was always talking.
I tried to show I cared.
I told him he meant much to me,
but he just sat and stared.

He needed so to listen,
to hear about my Lord.
It troubled me for I could see
that he was always bored.

But now I sit here listening,
to this preacher boy admit,
That boy I thought was hearing naught,
heard everything I did.

7. Galatians 1:11-12 "For I would have you know, brethren, that the gospel which was preached by me is not according to man. For I neither received it from man, nor was I taught it, but I received it through a revelation of Jesus Christ."

## **DELIVER THE SERMON**

Many sermons in many places I've preached.
All from God's Word were delivered.
I expect very few are remembered.
I hold hope of some needy hearts reached.

In a year 52 sermons presented,
Taking great care to cover essentials:
Spiritual gifts, spiritual growth, Christian principles.
Every truth, every doctrine defended.

We seldom at the time know the impact,
If real change was begun and real growth,
Encouragement or enlightenment or both.
Giving hearts hope and love they have lacked.

We prepare and deliver the sermon,
Believing every Scripture, every verse.
Having faith spiritual encounter occurs,
While convinced only time will determine.

CHAPTER FIVE

# PRAYER

John 16:23-24 "Truly, truly, I say to you, if you ask the Father for anything in My name, He will give it to you. Until now you have asked for nothing in My name; ask and you will receive, so that your joy may be made full."

All who are involved in Christian ministries know the absolute importance of bathing everything we do in prayer. We not only want to pray because we have a love relationship with our Lord and our Savior, but also find ourselves driven to prayer as we recognize our absolute dependence on God's leadership, direction, provision, and wisdom to accomplish the mission to which we have been called.

Praying is an activity about which there are differing opinions and many questions. Do we have to close our eyes and bow our heads? Children ask me that. Must we end the prayer with "Amen"? Must we cross ourselves after we pray? Can we pray to our deceased loved ones? Are there things we should not request from God? Is it okay to repeat the same words each time we pray? If we do it wrong, does it nullify our prayer requests?

With regard to that last question, let me ask another. When you go to your earthly parent or grandparent, do you have to be careful what you ask for or how you say it? If your answer is "no," then why? If you have a loving relationship with that parent or grandparent, you know you can talk to them about anything and everything without worrying about how you say it. Your communications are tied to your relationship. Our prayers to God, our Father, are also.

Jesus did not command us to pray. He did, however, ask us to pray in faith and with persistence. I recommend you read chapter ten in my book, *Commandments of Jesus*. He gave us a model prayer that begins, "Our Father, who art in heaven." And He told His followers "If you ask anything in My name; He will give it to you" (John 16:23). I choose to pray to my Father and close my prayer with, "In Jesus name I pray, Amen."

1. Psalm 51:10-12 "Create in me a clean heart, O God, and renew a steadfast spirit within me. Do not cast me away from Your presence and do not take your Holy Spirit from me. Restore to me the joy of Your salvation and sustain me with a willing spirit."

## REMAKING MY HEART

A peaceful, restful, quiet hour,
    Away from work and worry,
Away from all that saps my power,
    From all the push and hurry.
For just a while may heaven's choir,
    Uplift and upward carry,
Rekindling the inward fire,
    Remaking my heart merry.

I need to hear my Father speaking
    With majesty and wonder,
A quiet, calming voice I'm seeking,
    Not flashing light and thunder,

Assuring words like, "Not forsaken,"
    And, "I am your defender,"
Will stir my soul to re-awaken,
    Remaking my heart tender.

2. Matthew 6:6 "But you, when you pray, go into your inner room, close your door and pray to your Father who is in secret, and your Father who sees what is done in secret will reward you."

## I NEED TO TALK

Sometimes when I am low, those times occasionally come.
The times when I am all alone, no song to sing or hum.
My spirit has been broken, my energy is gone.
I need someone to love me, someone to lean upon.
Someone to listen to me and always understand.
And when I cannot do a task, they'll lend a helping hand.

Dear Lord, I need somebody. But wait! That someone's You.
It's You who really love me no matter what I do,
On Your shoulders I can lean, and if I need to talk,
You'll listen and then through the day together we can walk.
Dear Lord, I'll always love You. I want to prove my love.
Please tell me now what I can do as You I'm thinking of?

Dear God, I hear Your answer. I'll do my very best.
To tell the old, old story will ever be my quest.
And when I find someone who's low like I have been today,
I'll tell them how Your saving power can help them on their way.
Dear Lord, I close this prayer now. Forgive me of my sin.
Guide me through each precious day. In Jesus name, Amen!

3. Psalm 73:21-24 "When my heart was embittered and I was pierced within, then I was senseless and ignorant; I was like a beast before You. Nevertheless, I am continually with You; You have taken hold of my right hand, with Your counsel You will guide me and afterward receive me to glory."

## I HOLD OUT MY HAND

I hold out my hand, O Lord, for Thine.
    I need Thy help today.
My strength is waning, almost gone.
    My need is great, I can't go on,
Without Thy hand embracing mine.

I hold out my hand, O Lord, please take it.
    One hand I lift to Thee.
Your strength is strengthening the other
    by which I hold onto my brother.
When you hold mine, we both can make it.

I hold out my hand, O Lord, enfold.
    I'll never draw it back.
Without your strength I'll always fail.
    The one I try to help as well.
His hope relies upon our hold.

4. Matthew 19:14 "And Jesus said, 'Let the children alone, and do not hinder them from coming to Me; for the kingdom of heaven belongs to such as these.'"

## THE SWEETEST SOUND

Oh, the sweet sound of a spring rain coming,

Or the dew drops in the early morn,
The gentle sound of mother humming,
And the bird's song after summer's storm,
The sound of tall old windmills whirring,
Or the busy buzzing of the bees,
And the sound of playful kittens purring,
Or a soft breeze blowing through the trees.

I know these sounds are soft and sweet,
Very precious to the ear,
And I know this list is incomplete,
There are others as sweet to hear,
But the times when most my heart was stirred
Were at times when my head was bowed.
For the sweetest sound I have ever heard
Was the sound of a praying child.

5. Psalm 63:1-8 "O God, You are my God; I shall seek You earnestly; My soul thirsts for You, my flesh yearns for You, in a dry and weary land where there is no water. Thus I have seen You in the sanctuary, to see Your power and Your glory, because Your lovingkindness is better than life, my lips will praise You. So I will bless You as long as I live; I will lift up my hands in Your name. My soul is satisfied as with marrow and fatness, and my mouth offers praises with joyful lips. When I remember You on my bed, I meditate on You in the night watches. For You have been my help, and in the shadow of Your wings I sing for joy. My soul clings to You; Your right hand upholds me."

## A DESERT PRAYER
### (during Desert Storm with 4th Marine Regiment)

Why a desert Lord?
Why create a place

with so much space,
where rows and rows
of nothing grows?
Could it be here,
In this sandy shelf,
I will find myself,
lacking a view,
but closer to you?

6. Matthew 6:9 "Pray then in this way: Our Father who is in heaven, hallowed be Your name." John 14:13 "Whatever you ask in My name, that will I do, so that the Father may be glorified in the Son."

## HOW TO PRAY

Lesson One: Remember!
    Our King and Lord of all
        We humbly are addressing.
    Before His throne we call
        For undeserved blessing.

Lesson Two: Remember!
    As Father He invites.
        With loving heart, He hears.
    And in His presence quiets
        Our trembling souls and fears.

Lesson Three: Remember!
    Our prayers should each include
        A pledge to for Him live.
    With want for love renewed,
        Not just what He can give.

Lesson Four: Remember!
    Our right to stand before
        The God of all creation:
    In Jesus name our prayer.
        In Him our right relation.

7. Daniel 6:10 "… and he continued kneeling on his knees three times a day, praying and giving thanks before his God, as he had been doing previously."

## MY EVENING PRAYERS

I often lie awake at night,
    deprived of the Land of Nod.
And conclude the extra time just right
    to use to talk to God.

My evening prayers are open ended.
    I pray, and pray to sleep,
Then wake, my earlier prayer amended,
    Then sleep, then pray. Repeat.

Sometimes I, during dream or REM,
    awake with words from God.
Attributed by me to Him.
    Some people call that odd.

But knowing I'd forget by morn,
    I up and write them down.
I write the words my sleep has born,
    then back to bed I bound.

I offer now some proof to show

>     The truth of what I've said.
> This poem began some nights ago
>     From words God gave in bed.

8. 1 Samuel 3:9-10 "And Eli said to Samuel, 'Go lie down, and it shall be if He calls you, that you shall say, 'Speak Lord, for Your servant is listening.' So, Samuel went and lay down in his place. Then the Lord came and stood and called as at other times, 'Samuel! Samuel!' And Samuel said, 'Speak, for Your servant is listening.'"

## PRAYING SOME MORE

I start the day rushing, not much time to pray,
>     A quick prayer, and then out the door.
But a yellow line road, and slow car in my way,
>     God provides time for praying some more.

I always remember to pray at each meal.
>     I recite what I'm so thankful for.
But later I'm faced with some down-time to fill,
>     Perfect timing for praying some more.

One might think peculiar how my prayer life seems,
>     Depending on times when I'm bored.
But I am more taken by what it all means,
>     That I love spending time with my Lord.

Sometimes I lie restless, not falling to sleep.
>     I helplessly reason just why.
I finally ask, when I stop counting sheep,
>     "Dear Lord, if it's you, here am I."

CHAPTER SIX

# THE GOSPEL OF JESUS CHRIST

Romans 10:9-10 "…that if you confess with your mouth the Lord Jesus and believe in your heart that God has raised Him from the dead, you will be saved, for with the heart one believes unto righteousness, and with the mouth confession is made unto salvation."

I object to the idea that every ministry or even any Christian ministry is only done for the purpose of having opportunity to share the gospel. This thinking leads inevitably to a position that any ministry of the church that doesn't share the gospel is a waste of the church's efforts and budget. In my opinion, this thinking undervalues the Christians' acts of love and considers them only deceitful efforts to persuade the lost to believe. We can't ignore Ephesians 2:10, "For we are His workmanship, created in Christ Jesus for good works, which God prepared beforehand so that we would walk in them."

Having said that, I do believe that every Christian ministry should be carried out with Christ-like love that cares not only for meeting physical, emotional and educational needs, but also for every person's spiritual needs. Sharing the Gospel should be a natural and un-coerced behavior in ministry.

The gospel of Jesus Christ was proclaimed by angels to shepherds in the field. This was and is the Good News: "I bring you good tidings of great joy which will be to all the people. For there is born to you this day in the city of David a Savior who is Christ the Lord" (Luke 2:10-11). We understand this gospel/good news message as it is simply communicated to Nicodemus in these sweet words from Jesus' lips. "For God so loved the world that He gave His only begotten Son, that whoever believes in Him should not perish but have everlasting life" (John 3:16).

Every Christian minister should be eagerly able to confess with Paul. "For I am not ashamed of the gospel, for it is the power of God for salvation to everyone who believes, to the Jew first and also to the Greek" (Romans 1:16). We are not ashamed of the gospel, neither are we afraid to share it.

1. Matthew 27:28-31 "They stripped Him and put a scarlet robe on Him, and after twisting together a crown of thorns, they put it on His head, and a reed in His right hand; and they knelt down before Him and mocked Him saying, 'Hail, King of the Jews!' They spat on Him, and took the reed and began to beat Him on the head. After they had mocked Him, they took the scarlet robe off Him and put His own garments back on Him and led Him away to crucify Him."

## ASHAMED?

Ashamed is not what Jesus was
    when from glory He descended.
He took a human form because
    It was what God intended.

Ashamed is not what Jesus was
    when He walked from place to place.
He humbly lived without applause,
    just depending on God's grace.

Ashamed is not what Jesus was
    when He wore that crown of thorns,
When He suffered spitting, beating, plus
    all the crowds' contempt and scorn.

Ashamed is not what Jesus was
    when He died for all my sin.
And I will not one moment pause
    to be ashamed of loving Him.

2. John 19:28-30 "After this, Jesus, knowing that all things had already been accomplished, to fulfill the Scripture, said, 'I am thirsty.' A jar full of sour wine was standing there; so they put a sponge full of the sour wine upon a branch of hyssop and brought it up to His mouth. Therefore when Jesus had received the sour wine, He said, 'It is finished!' And He bowed His head and gave up His spirit."

### "IT" IS A WORD

"It" is (as you will see) a word
with emblematic meaning.
A word is "it" and it a word
with truth well worth revealing.

When closely viewed, I will allude,
we see our likeness in "it."
"It" pictures we who live by grace,
so now let me present "it."

"It" starts with just a little "i."
That's me or you who stands there,
And we are standing by the "T,"
The cross of Christ our Savior.

Now seeing "it" for what it is
We sing a constant chorus,
To stand beside where Jesus died.
Where Jesus suffered for us.

"It" is a picture of our life,
With Jesus "it" is cherished,
Recalling words He spoke in death,
He told us "It is finished."

3. Matthew 11:28-30 "Come to Me, all who are weary and heavy-laden, and I will give you rest. Take My yoke upon you and learn from Me, for I am gentle and humble in heart, and you will find rest for your souls. For My yoke is easy and My burden is light."

## COME UNTO ME

"Come unto me"
I speak the words my Jesus spoke,
His presence I invoke,
His mercy, love and grace.

"Come unto me"
And lay your heavy burdens down,
And watch that awful frown,
Become a smiling face.

"Come unto me"
And we will try to lift your load,
And set you on the road,
That leads to sanity.

"Come unto me"
And let us take away your crutch.
Our God cares very much
About humanity.

"Come unto me"
And we will go to God in prayer,
And leave our burdens there,
To trust His Holy power.

"Come unto me"
And pour out all your pain and grief,
And God will send relief
Within this very hour.

4. Luke 3:3-4 "And he [John the Baptist] came into all the district around the Jordan, preaching a baptism of repentance for the forgiveness of sins; as it is written in the book of the words of Isaiah the prophet, "The voice of one crying in the wilderness, 'Make ready the way of the Lord, make His paths straight. Every ravine will be filled, and every mountain and hill will be brought low; the crooked will become straight, and the rough roads smooth; and all flesh will see the salvation of God.'"

## GONNA BUILD A HIGHWAY

Going to build a highway
    to the heart of men.
Going to build a highway
    for the Lord to come in.
Going to make real smooth,
    that new highway.
Cause a king is coming,

        Who is going to change our night today!

Going to level mountains,
        and going to fill the valleys.
Going to tell about Jesus,
        down the streets and alleys.
Going to straighten out
        the crooked road,
Cause a King is coming,
        Who is going to lift our heavy load.

Going to build a highway,
        And it's up to me,
Just to build a highway
        for the world to see,
Of the Lord's salvation,
        and the peace it brings.
Cause the King is coming,
        And His name is Jesus, King of Kings!

5. Psalm 23:1-3 "The Lord is my shepherd, I shall not want. He makes me lie down in green pastures; He leads me beside quiet waters, He restores my soul; He guides me in the paths of righteousness for His name's sake."

## GREEN PASTURES AND STILL WATERS

I love green pastures and still waters.
        I love still more the master.
I know when following close to him,
        He leads me from disaster.

A pasture lush I'm lying down in,
    Abundantly He feeds me,
Beside the ever-flowing fountain,
    A loving shepherd leads me.

My God is ever good to those who
    Take the path He chooses,
And all shall never want for more whose
    Shepherd is Lord Jesus.

If any find themselves untended,
    Lost and needing rescue,
Turn round your life with hand extended,
    Take Jesus' hand, He'll save you!

6. Luke 18:18 "A ruler questioned Him, saying, 'Good Teacher, what shall I do to inherit eternal life?'"

## IF I WERE A RICH MAN

"If I were a rich man," Tevye
From "Fiddler on the Roof" would say,
"If rich, I'd finally have the time.
To sit in synagogues and pray."

But when the rich young ruler came
To ask of Christ a question,
It seems a young and wealthy man
Faces costly indecision.

The question was, "What must I do,
That I may gain eternal life?"
The answer Jesus gave to him,

Caused heart distress and strife.

"One thing you lack, sell all you have,"
And after, "come and follow me."
He sorrowful could not comply,
For very rich a man was he.

Tevye's song ends, "Would I if rich
Spoil some immense eternal plan?"
Perhaps you would not follow Jesus,
If you were a wealthy man.

7. Matthew 7:13,14 "Enter by the narrow gate; for the gate is wide and the way is broad that leads to destruction, and there are many who enter through it. For the gate is small and the way is narrow that leads to life, and there are few who find it."

The Roman Road: Romans 3:10, 3:23, 5:8, 6:23, 10:9, and 10:13

## ROMAN ROAD TO SALVATION

The road to destruction has appeal,
While the pathway to life seems unkind.
Many will travel the pathway to hell,
And the road to true life few will find.

The road to hell offers false joy,
At the end of that road is great sorrow.
The road to true life leads to glory,
With hope for today and tomorrow.

All sinned and fell short of God's glory.
For sins it is death that God gives us.

But His love is made clear in our story.
While sinners, His Son died to save us.

Declare God's Son Jesus is Lord!
Believe from the dead God has raised Him,
To pay a price that we can't afford,
In our heart with our mouth let us praise Him!

Trust Jesus now, don't delay!
For the road to destruction is paved –
With intentions to trust Him some day.
Call on Him now and be saved!

CHAPTER SEVEN

# BIBLE STORIES

Hebrews 11:32-34 "And what more shall I say? For time will fail me if I tell of Gideon, Barak, Samson, Jephthah, of David and Samuel and the prophets, who by faith conquered kingdoms, performed acts of righteousness, obtained promises, shut the mouths of lions, quenched the power of fire, escaped the edge of the sword, from weakness were made strong, became mighty in war, put foreign armies to flight,"

The faith stories are some of the best Bible stories. In the Scripture above, the writer of Hebrews could have added some New Testament names like Peter, Paul, and Mary. We love all those stories. They encourage us, inspire us, and even shame us. When we fail in our walk of faith and allow doubt to restrain us, we remember the storm scene, with a boat load of disciples, and we hear our Lord's words to them saying, "Why are you fearful, O you of little faith?' (Matthew 8:25).

Some of our best sermons, Bible studies, and children's lessons focus on those faith heroes. Their names are connected in our minds to memorable mottos: "Dare to be a Daniel," "Made for such a time as this" (Esther), "Be a giant slayer (David), "The patience of Job," and "A man after my own heart" (David). These stories are also familiar to non-believers. No matter what ministry we have, inserting a Bible story into a conversation can create an opportunity to talk about faith and to ask individuals about their own faith or lack of it.

While Jesus questioned a crowd, "Why are you worried about clothing?" He directed their attention to the lilies of the field and introduced into the conversation a name all would recognize. "Not even Solomon in all his glory clothed himself like one of these" (Matthew 6:29). On another occasion Jesus was asked for a sign. His answer was, "no sign will be given except for the sign of Jonah." The Pharisees didn't understand that warning sign to the Ninevites. Jesus smoothly transitioned the story of Job from a warning to the familiar story of the big fish. "Just as Jonah was three days and three nights in the belly of the sea monster, so will the Son of Man be three days and three nights in the heart of the earth" (Matthew 12:40).

The quick and clever thinking minister can always bring an occasion-fitting Bible story into a dialogue regardless of the particular persons present. The unexpected introduction of a Bible story for discussion immediately introduces a dynamic that may become a spiritual explosion. Our commitment to ministry is a commitment to teaching moments and their ever-present possibilities.

1. Genesis 50:24 "And Joseph said to his brethren, 'I am dying, but God will surely visit you and bring you out of this land to the land of which He swore to Abraham, to Isaac, and to Jacob.'"

## **MOSES**

Israelites multiplying.
In fear of future fighting,
The king said kill all baby boys.
God's people started crying.

A mother and mister,
And a little baby's sister,
Wrapped up the newborn baby boy

To hide their precious treasure.

A tisket, a tasket,
Young Moses in a basket.
He floated down the river Nile.
His mother thought she lost it.

She took it, from the water.
She was the Pharoah's daughter.
She took the baby home as hers,
Now Pharoah his grandfather.

God's answer to our praying,
When faithfully we are faithing,
Comes always with God's perfect timing.
God is working, not delaying.

A burning bush, Moses God's man,
Ten plagues, the killing of a lamb,
Yada, Yada, Yada.
God's people led to promised land.

2.1 Kings 19:11-12 "And after the wind an earthquake, but the Lord was not in the earthquake. After the earthquake a fire, but the Lord was not in the fire; and after the fire a sound of a gentle blowing."

## EARS ENGAGED

A tiny mouse squeaks, next to crows,
Ark spilling rows by rows.
Some happy birds chirp,
With glimpse of a rainbow.
Ark's animals leave, like rebirth

Completing God's cleansing of earth.

With Bible in hand, we explore,
Truth mining more and more.
Read without speeding,
Through each Scripture story,
With eyes and two ears engaged,
We capture much more from each page.

Goliath came tumbling down,
From Philistines not a sound
David was faithful,
God's victory profound.
Imagine the shouts and the praise,
God's people were making those days.

If any have ears let him hear.
God's Word is very clear.
Not hearing's absurd,
Soon we will be hearing,
If all other voices ignored,
The still quiet voice of the Lord.

3. John 1:35-36 "Again, the next day, John was standing with two of his disciples, and he looked at Jesus as He walked, and said, 'Behold the Lamb of God!'"

## MARY HAD A LITTLE LAMB

She gave to God a mother's womb,
To bear her Lord and Savior.
Mary had a little lamb,
And laid Him in a manger.

Mary, hold your little man,
While He is in your care.
Soon His Father's perfect plan
Becomes His cross to bear.

Mary had a little lamb.
The lamb was born to die,
Providing us and Jesus' mom,
By grace, through faith, to life.

4. Genesis 28:12 "He had a dream, and behold, a ladder was set on the earth with its top reaching to heaven; and behold, the angels of God were ascending and descending on it."

## JACOB'S DREAM

Isaac sent Him on a trip.
Ole Jacob traveled all alone.
When sundown came he went to sleep,
His head at rest upon a stone.

He dreamed while lying on the ground,
A ladder with a multitude
Of angels going up and down,
And high above Jehovah stood.

Said The Lord, "Where you now rest
I give you and your ancestry.
In you will all the earth be blessed,
For I with you will always be."

Jacob's vision was so clear,
A dream that time could not erase.

"I did not know the Lord is here,
Wow! This is such an awesome place!"

"Bethel now will be the name,
God's house must occupy this plot,"
And with a vow the Lord he claimed,
A rock was raised to mark the spot.

5. 2 Kings 20:9-10 "Isaiah said, 'This shall be the sign to you from the Lord, that the Lord will do the thing that He has spoken; shall the shadow go forward ten steps or go back ten steps?' So Hezekiah answered, 'It is easy for the shadow to decline ten steps; no, but let the shadow turn backward ten steps.'"

## A LIMERICK ON HEZEKIAH

There once was a king Hezekiah,
Who was ill and God said he would die ah,
But Isaiah he say ah:
"You'll not die on this day ah,
For God hears me and you when we cry ah."

Continuing this attempt to be lyrical,
For a sign God used something spherical.
He backed up the sun,
And when he was done,
Hezekiah was healed, 'twas a miracle.

Was there a Mount Hezekiah?
Located near the land of Moriah?
Some have often mis-took
Him to be a Bible book,
In between Haggai and Zephaniah.

6. Genesis 3:4-5 "The serpent said to the woman, 'You surely will not die! For God knows that in the day you eat of it your eyes will be opened, and you will be like God, knowing good and evil.'"

## THE SERPENT LIED

The serpent lied.
"That fruit you eyed
Is truth denied."
"Your eyes," he cried,
"Will open wide
No one has died
Who this fruit tried."
So, Eve complied.
Then testified
At Adam's side.
He gratified
His carnal side.
Then tried to hide,
But he God spied,
And clothed with hide,
Then both were tried,
Sin set aside.
From Paradise,
Disqualified.
And all men died.
Sin multiplied.
Then God supplied
A Lamb who died,
Was crucified.
On Him relied
Those justified,
God glorified,
His chosen bride.

6. Mark 10:13-14 "And they were bringing children to Him so that He might touch them; but the disciples rebuked them. But when Jesus saw this, He was indignant and said to them, 'Permit the children to come to Me; do not hinder them; for the kingdom of God belongs to such as these.'"

## ALL ARE PRECIOUS IN HIS SIGHT

Only someone who was there
    could fathom the love that flowed.
Never could one know the warmth
    Just hearing the story told.
Love like His, mere human words
    could never pretend to paint,
The beauty of His tenderness
    While spurning ill complaint.

Jesus bid the children come,
    And not be sent away.
They came, He blessed them everyone,
    Letting them laugh and play.
He was bothered not, that all of them
    Now made a little noise.
He didn't expect them to behave,
    Except as girls and boys.

Still, He seeks to love the small
    To be their guiding Light,
To love all children of the world,
    Red, yellow, black and white.
And we must be His loving arms,
    Inviting all to come.
That through our aid, and care, and love,
    He'll bless them everyone.

CHAPTER EIGHT

# LOVING PEOPLE

Matthew 22:36-40 "Teacher, which is the great commandment in the Law? And He said to him, 'You shall love the Lord your God with all your heart, and with all your soul, and with all your mind. This is the great and foremost commandment. The second is like it, you shall love your neighbor as yourself. On these two commandments depend the whole law and the Prophets.'"

ఈ∾ఈ

Our work in Christian ministry is with people. All people. God sent His Son because He "so loved the world." Our ministry is to love people in the name of Jesus. That ministry of love is expressed through caring for people, supporting them, encouraging them, and teaching them that God loves them. Archie Headley was my pastor many years ago. I don't remember anything that he preached or taught except that he always ended the Sunday morning service by saying, "God loves you and so do I." If people hear nothing else from us, they should at least hear that.

If you do <u>not</u> love people, then you should not be engaged in Christian ministry. John the Apostle wrote, "Beloved, let us love one another, for love is from God; and everyone who loves is born of God and knows God. The one who does not love does not know God, for God is love" (1 John 4:7-8). There are Christian ministers who love to preach and teach but who have great difficulty loving people. John provides a test of our love. "We know love by this, that He laid down His life for us; and we ought to lay down our lives for the brethren. But whoever has the world's goods, and sees his brother in need, and closes his heart against him, how does the love of God abide in him?" (1 John 3:16-17).

If we are ministers of Jesus Christ, surely, we will mimic the love Jesus showed for people. In chapter five of my book *Commandments of Jesus*, I wrote this: "We are to love others like Jesus loves them. He loves the lame, the maimed, the blind, the demon-possessed, the sick, the leper, the ones who disappointed Him, the ones who betrayed Him, and the ones who deserted Him, and He loves me." If we cannot love them, we cannot minister to them. If we love them as Jesus loves them, they will eventually understand that Jesus loves them. That is our ministry mission.

1. Matthew 25:19-21 "Now after a long time the master of those slaves came and settled accounts with them. The one who had received the five talents came up and brought five more talents, saying, 'Master, you entrusted five talents to me. See, I have gained five more talents.' His master said to him, 'Well done, good and faithful slave, you were faithful with a few things. I will put you in charge of many things; enter into the joy of your master.'"

## TO SERVE YOU WELL

Dear Lord, I love the work You gave me,
But, many times I fail
To do my best boldly and bravely.
I want to serve You well.

I need to better know Your people,
To fully understand,

When they are strong or growing feeble,
So, I can hold their hand.

I fail to show enough affection
To prove my "I love you!"
And often offer strong correction,
When softer words would do.

Developing their understanding
Has been a little slow.
Perhaps I should be more demanding,
Exhorting them to grow.

Forgive me when I let sheep wander,
Not keeping careful guard.
Some hours I severely squander,
Not working very hard.

I love to labor, Lord and Master,
Instruct me that I may,
Persistently improve as pastor,
Until my dying day.

2. Romans 8:38-39 "For I am convinced that neither death, nor life, nor angels, nor principalities, nor things present, nor things to come, nor powers, nor height, nor depth, nor any other created thing, will be able to separate us from the love of God, which is in Christ Jesus our Lord."

## MY ATTITUDE OF OTHERS

Is my attitude of others based
upon their nice appearance?

Does each person passing by receive
a scrutinizing clearance?
And then afterward I favor those
who passed my stern inspections,
While I treat the others rudely for
their body imperfections?

I have come to see how wrong I've been
in basing my decision,
Of whom I will accept, upon
their physical condition.
And, I am now persuaded that
from now and for forever:

Neither bad breath, nor jive, nor strange smells,
nor limited faculties, nor wearing apparel,
nor sins present, nor sins to come, nor height,
nor width, nor any other feature
shall be able to deviate me from loving others
with the Love of God!

3. Ephesians 4:1-2 "Therefore I, the prisoner of the Lord, implore you to walk in a manner worthy of the calling with which you have been called, with all humility and gentleness, with patience, showing tolerance for one another in love, …"

## HUMILITY, GENTLENESS, AND PATIENCE

An argument starts, or just continues,
Breaking hearts and bones and sinews.
Rarely civil, never ending.
On the brink of beyond mending.
Curse the pride that fans the fire.

Curse the ever-deepening mire.
Three things conquer pride's creations:
Humility, gentleness, and also patience.

One drink began a loathsome journey,
Ending on a cold basement gurney.
No cry for help, no quiet contrition,
No addiction to alcohol admission.
Curse the pride that hides the pain.
Curse the choice to die in vain.
Three things break up pride's fixations:
Humility, gentleness, and also patience.

When pride arrives, disgrace comes too (Proverbs 11:2)
The pride of heart will always deceive you. (Jeremiah 49:16)
Pride breeds quarrels, precedes a fall. (Proverbs 13:10; 16:18)
It doesn't leave God any room at all. (Psalm 10:4)
God hates the arrogant, hates the proud. (Proverbs 8:3)
God hates and will punish this unholy crowd. (Proverbs 16:5)
Three things find in chapter 6 of Galatians:
Humility, gentleness, and also patience.

4. 2 Thessalonians 1:2-3 "Grace to you and peace from God the Father and the Lord Jesus Christ. We ought always to give thanks to God for you brethren, as is only fitting, because your faith is greatly enlarged, and the love of each one of you toward one another grows ever greater; …"

## THE CARE GIVER TREASURE

Here comes Betty walking near me,
Here comes Thomas, there sits John,
Anne, and Alfred, Margie, Elsie,

Seeing them, though they're all gone.

Life provides an endless mixture,
Scenes scroll like a movie show,
Watching reels of old, old pictures,
Mem'ries etched on heart and soul.

Moving on, though ne'er erasing;
Living in the now instead.
Other elders daily tracing,
Precious scenes inside my head.

Can the heart be over loaded,
Reach a point too full to care?
At the brim and over running -
No more space for mem'ries there?

May our chests hold endless measures.
Lord, when cups fill up to brims,
Make them so to hold more treasures -
Precious jewels and sparkling gems.

5. Ephesians 3:20 "Now to Him who is able to do far more abundantly beyond all that we ask or think; according to the power that works within us, to Him be the glory in the church and in Christ Jesus to all generations forever and ever. Amen."

## ANYTHING CAN HAPPEN

Him? Oh no!
Not that bad boy,
He could never be

>A person who would wind up with
>>His name in history.

Her? Not her!
A Governor?
That's a hopeless dream,
>To think that slow poke girl could ever
>>Build up that much steam.

Me? Oh my!
Afraid to try?
What a thing to say,
>I know that anything can happen
>>By God's work and way.

Them? All them?
Okay. For Him!
He who died for me.
>I'll tell them how with Jesus they have
>>Life abundantly.

Him? and her?
How I wonder,
What their life will be?
>I know anything can happen.
>>Jesus is the key!

6. 1 Corinthians 13:7,8 "[Love] bears all things, believes all things, hopes all things, endures all things. Love never fails;…"

## **A YOUNG MAN**

Here sits a young man,

Angry and bitter,
He has rebelled against life's normal stream.
He has his own plan,
Labelled a quitter,
He still pursues some impossible dream.

His one request is -
Note not his presence,
Why can't reality leave him alone?
People repress his
Singular essence,
He is a being who needs not be known.

Still, I can win him,
Though he denies it,
Though all attempts to explain are rebuffed.
Somewhere within him,
Though he disguise it,
He has a definite need to be loved.

All his defenses
Won't last forever,
Sooner or later I can't be denied
Slowly by inches,
Winning his favor,
I cannot fail,
He has God on his side.

7. Proverbs 3:5-8 "Trust in the Lord with all your heart and do not lean on your own understanding. In all your ways acknowledge Him, and He will make your paths straight. Do not be wise in your own eyes; fear the Lord and turn away from evil. It will be healing to your body and refreshment to your bones."

## SEPARTION OR DIVORCE?

Separation or Divorce
Is too common today
among couples both old and new.
Because marriage is a course
unnavigable they say,
and love is no longer a glue.

Selfishness and stubbornness,
Is likely the cause
of arguments, quarrels, and misfits.
Inabilities to love others,
Are likely the flaws
That lead to misdeeds and bad habits.

Weekly church and Bible reading
Is a great source of healing,
A daily dose, my recommendation.
It might be too late
But it could be revealing,
And may provide great navigation.

Love, grace and mercy
Are rich healing lotions,
If amply applied to each other.
Apply them with prayer
To your heated emotions.
It may help your marriage recover.

CHAPTER NINE

# HEAVEN

2 Corinthians 5:1, 4-7 "For we know that if the earthly tent which is our house is torn down, we have a building from God, a house not made with hands, eternal in the heavens. ... For indeed while we are in this tent, we groan, being burdened, because we do not want to be unclothed but to be clothed, so that what is mortal will be swallowed up by life. Now He who prepared us for this very purpose is God, who gave to us the Spirit as a pledge. Therefore, being always of good courage, and knowing that while we are at home in the body we are absent from the Lord – For we walk by faith, not by sight."

When we are ministering for our Lord Jesus, no matter what the capacity, we sometimes find ourselves pulled in two directions. Ministry can tire us so much, as we spend ourselves helping difficult people, that we sometimes long to leave this earth and go home to heaven. At the same time, enjoying the people and work of ministry God has given us, we can't imagine quitting. Not yet!

The groaning mentioned in 2 Corinthians above is part of the pull in two directions Paul describes in Philippians 1:21-24. "For to me, to live is Christ and to die is gain. But if I am to live on in the flesh, this will mean fruitful labor for me; and I do not know which to choose. But I am hard-pressed from both directions, having the desire to depart and be with Christ, for that is very much better; yet to remain on in the flesh is more necessary for your sake."

That is the groaning we each sometimes feel. I think Paul would admit that the decision of whether to live or die is not up to us. I love the words of the old hymn "We'll Work Till Jesus Comes," written by Elizabeth Mills: "O land of rest, for thee I sigh! When will the moment come when I shall lay my armor by and dwell in peace at home?" Yes! We know that feeling, and yet we also have an undying commitment. We will work until Jesus comes or until He calls us home.

1. Matthew 6:9 "Our Father who is in heaven, Hallowed be Your name."

## HE IS MY FATHER

I am His son, and He is my Father.
    Adopted, yet I am an heir to His throne.
Though not at first, I became through believing,
    Part of His family, He calls me His own.

God of my faith You are author and finisher,
    Thanks to Jesus forever I'm Yours.
More than creator and giver of life to me,
    You are my Father on Heavenly shores.

I long to be with my Father in heaven.
    One of these days, maybe soon, there I'll be.
There in His glorious Heavenly Kingdom,
    Always together, my Father and me.

2. Revelation 22:3-4 "There will no longer be any curse; and the throne of God and of the Lamb will be in it, and His bond servants will serve Him; they will see His face, and His name will be on their foreheads."

## I LONG FOR HEAVEN

I long for heaven, it is my dream.
Like wish to fish each time I pass
A pond or stream.

I long for heaven when changes curse.
No hymns are sung and baby grand,
Not played in church.

I long for heaven when war begins,
Or hearing lies, or someone dies,
Or marriage ends.

I long for heaven whenever Dad,
And others missed turn thoughts to tears,
And semblance sad.

I long for heaven as face and hand,
So aged look, my soul prepares
For Beulah land.

I long for heaven to leave this place,
And be with God to hold His hand,
And see His face.

3. John 14:3 "If I go and prepare a place for you, I will come again and receive you to Myself, that there I am, there you may be also."

## BEHOLD MY JESUS

Just watch and wait,
the day is nearing,
God set a date
for Christ's appearing,
In midnight dream
I look for something,
Some future scenes
Of Jesus coming.

I wait and watch,
and in my wonder,
Long for relief
from trials I'm under,
Where is my Lord,
my strength is dying.
Has he not heard
my prayer, my crying.

But look a gate
in heav'n has opened,
A shining light,
the darkness broken,
The sky is stirred
but still a calmness.
Behold God's word,
behold God's promise.

Behold God's grace,
unmerited favor,
Behold the face
of my dear savior,

God's people sing,
God's people praising,
Behold the King,
God's love amazing!

Behold the King
the one who frees us.
My everything,
behold my Jesus!
And as from sleep,
I wake in wonder.
I crave God's call
To come up yonder.

4. 1 Thessalonians 4:13-14 "But we do not want you to be uninformed, brethren, about those who are asleep, so that you will not grieve as do the rest who have no hope. For if we believe that Jesus died and rose again, even so God will bring with Him those who have fallen asleep in Jesus."

## **GIVE ME A SIMPLE FUNERAL**

Bury me in a plain box.
Don't put me in some satin-lined case,
Adorned with copper, silver and lace.
No costly casket transports to that place
Where I'll forever behold my Lord's face.
Bury me in a plain box!

Bury me in an old suit.
I won't be pleased or even impressed,
If I am preserved and splendidly dressed.
Don't dress me up like some dinner guest,

Those fancy clothes won't make me more blessed.
Bury me in an old suit!

Give me a simple funeral.
Don't labor long with my eulogy,
Consuming moments with memories of me.
Just praise my Lord for His sovereignty.
And care for and comfort my family.
Give me a simple funeral!

Bury me quickly.
Don't lay some flowers each year by my bed,
My bones can't see if they're white, pink or red.
Life's far too short to waste on the dead,
Move on to joys of living instead.
Bury me quickly!

5. Revelation 19:5-7 "And a voice came from the throne, saying, 'Give praise to our God, all you His bond-servants, you who fear Him, the small and the great.' Then I heard something like the voice of a great multitude and like the sound of many waters and like the sound of mighty peals of thunder, saying, 'Hallelujah! For the Lord our God, the Almighty, reigns.'"

## NO ONE KNOWS

No one knows the time and place
    a shower shall descend from space.
No one knows the spot or hour
    planned to welcome some new flower.

No one knows why different colors
    adorn the backs of global brothers.

No one knows if people are
    on some yet undiscovered star.

No one knows where Adam's boys
    went to find their female choice.
Was the fruit Eve ate a lemon?
    Why are men outlived by women?

Though we may surmise a little,
    Many things remain a riddle.
Do not fret, God never fails us.
    What we need to know God tells us.

Someday when we live up yonder,
    If these questions you still ponder,
While we sing a joyful chorus,
    you can ask the questions for us.

6. Romans 5:13-14 "For until the Law sin was in the world, but sin is not imputed when there is no law. Nevertheless, death reigned from Adam until Moses, even over those who had not sinned in the likeness of the offense of Adam, who is a type of Him who was to come."

## A CONVERSATION WITH ADAM

I have often had thoughts about heaven,
And with whom I'd like to implore,
    Some biblical person
    To find out their version,
To know just a little bit more.

I am hoping to talk with ole Adam,
Just a brief inquisition will do.

> Like, what first was Eve called
> when created by God?
Was she "bone of my bones" or "hey you?"

Please tell me what life with your wife was.
Was she smart, and carefree or confused?
> Did she bake apple pie?
> Was she apple of your eye?
Did she feel real important or used?

Was she miffed when you told God "That Woman!"
She, the reason you gave in to sin?
> The snake tale was odd,
> And you even blamed God,
Twas no way your sin to defend.

And, why did not Cain become shepherd?
Was it just that Cain never was Abel?
> Did you think Eve to blame
> For her raising such Cain?
These details are not in my Bible.

Of many things in heaven to fathom,
I'm hoping to talk with ole Adam.

7. Galatians 2:20 "I have been crucified with Christ; and it is no longer I who live, but Christ lives in me; and the life which I now live in the flesh I live by faith in the Son of God, who loved me and gave Himself up for me."

## WHAT DEATH?

I wonder what death I'll die, or in what way,
Or if I'll have a chance opining, "Oh, that's how?"
I wonder how long I'll live, one more day?
Or is it not in God's good timing to allow?

If somehow I suddenly die, unexpected,
And have no chance for my goodbyes. I hope not;
I hope that I will at least expect it,
Unless at night I'm attacked and stabbed and shot.

I wonder why I'm concerned about death;
Or, why I care how I'll be dying - by whose hand?
My number will not come up, not loss of breath,
Without my Lord's allowing, in His plan.

I'm going to die someday, somehow.
It might be pleasant, or violently, or eerily.
It will not happen today, no not now.
Today is my day to live, my God is near me.

CHAPTER TEN

# THE CHRISTIAN MINISTER'S FAMILY

1 Timothy 3:4 "He must be one who manages his own household well, keeping his children under control with all dignity (but if a man does not know how to manage his own household, how will he take care of the church of God?) …"

☙❧

In Christian ministry we fully understand the impact made on our family because of our service to God. We could not be effective without their support and without their support many ministers have found their ministry ineffective. I have known men and women who truly loved the Lord Jesus, and wished to serve Him well, but were hampered by, and even disabled by their un-supporting spouse, children, or parents.

Even Jesus had earthly family members who did not understand His purpose and probably questioned His ministry. Matthew 12 records an event where Jesus was speaking to a crowd and interrupted by His family. "Someone said to Him, 'Behold Your mother and Your brothers are standing outside seeking to speak to you'" (Matthew 12:47-50). Jesus responded to the messenger, "'Who is My mother and who are My brothers?' And stretching out His hand toward His disciples, He said, 'Behold My mother and My brothers! For whoever does the will of My Father who is in heaven he is My brother and sister and mother.'"

Christians in ministry understand this story. We have felt closer relationships with our partners in ministry and with those to whom we minister, than to our own family. That doesn't mean we have stopped loving our biological kin. Nor does it mean we are not responsible for their behavior. We absolutely must give time and attention to our spouse and children. They must know that we care for them as much and more than we care for the families under our ministry. We cannot let them be neglected and grow bitter and despise our devotion to ministry.

The Biblical example of a servant of God whose ministry was tainted by his children is Eli the high priest. In chapter two of 1 Samuel, two stories run side by side: The sweet story of Hannah presenting her son Samuel (the answer to her prayers) to Eli to serve in the house of God; and the sad story of Eli's sons ("now the sons of Eli were worthless men; they did not know the Lord" 1 Samuel 2:12). Though Eli faithfully served God and Israel as priest and judge for forty years, God judged him because of his sons. God spoke to Samuel about the matter. "For I have told him that I am about to judge his house forever for the iniquity which he knew, because his sons brought a curse on themselves and he did not rebuke them" (1 Samuel 3:13).

Paul's instructions concerning our children is as important for us as we serve in various ministries as it is for those to whom we teach God's word. "Fathers, do not provoke your children to anger, but bring them up in the discipline and instruction of the Lord" (Ephesians 6:4). We must cherish our wife and children! They are God's gifts to us. Whether they make or break our effectiveness in ministry may depend upon our loving care for them.

1. 2 Timothy 1:5 "For I am mindful of the sincere faith within you, which first dwelt in your grandmother Lois and your mother Eunice, and I am sure that it is in you as well."

## MY GRANDSON NORMAN
### By Evelyn Laeger Seago (Grandma)

There's a young man in my life 'Tis True
I've watched him grow from babe to man, I knew
At an early age there were signs of God's call
When you gave all you had to missions though gift was small.

I saw you teach the very young,
Your desire to lead them to Jesus, God's Son.
Also the challenge to work serve and play,
Teenagers to encourage along life's way.

There were years of loyalty to our country dear
To help bring peace and freedom from fear.
While there you saw the lonely, the careless, without spiritual sight.
Your eyes were open to their need of Christ – to show them THE LIGHT.

At just the right timing you met the girl of your dream.
Sweet Connie would be your helper – a perfect team.
There were years of hard study to prepare the way,
To be a minister, to serve God, be it night or day.

At last you became Chaplain and back to the Navy to answer God's call.
Your future is in His hands and with Him you'll never fall.
So, Grandson, my dear grandson, I love you for your wit and fun,
But, most of all for loving and serving Jesus, God's beloved Son.

2. Proverbs 14:26 "In the fear of the Lord there is strong confidence, and his children will have refuge."

## I TRUST THAT MY CHILDREN ARE SAFE

My children are your children always, dear Lord.
>They call You their Father, as they do me.

For love, strength and safety they look to us, Lord.
>A good, loving father are we.

I'm glad You are near my dear children tonight,
>I miss them and wish I was there; not here.

For now, I'm at sea and away from their sight.
>I trust You and need not to fear.

In dark, lonely nights I lift up thanks and praise,
>That You are, Dear Lord, by their side.

For You are not bound within time, skill, and space,
>And in You we safely abide.

And as I again lay my head down to sleep,
>I trust that my children are safe, at rest,

And our souls we trust in Your promise to keep,
>In You we forever are blest.

3. Proverbs 31:10-11 "Who can find a virtuous wife? For her worth is far above rubies. The heart of her husband safely trusts her; so he will have no lack of gain."

## ONE WONDERFUL WOMAN

I have found a virtuous woman,
She is truly one worthy of praise.
In this world I am sure there are few found,
So fully with God's love and grace.

Tender love she gives to her children,
Tender love is her middle name,
Tender love, she knows is fulfilled when
Given selflessly without any shame.

If I'm wrong, she gently corrects me.
If I'm right, my praise is her prayer.
If depressed, her presence uplifts me.
If excited, cheers fill the air.

When she smiles, my day becomes brighter.
When she laughs, clouds disappear.
When she prays, my load is much lighter.
When she cries, God sheds a tear.

God has given her patience and meekness.
She was given faith bountifully.
God was given great strength for my weakness.
She was specially made just for me.

God is truly a wonderful Master.
God gave me eternal life.
God gave me a calling to pastor,
Then gave me one wonderful wife.

4. Ephesians 5:25 "Husbands, love your wives, just as Christ also loved the church and gave Himself for her, …"

## MY WIFE FOUR YEARS YOUNGER THAN I

Where was I when my wife was formed
   within her mother's womb?
She, hushed, lie in her mother, warmed

while I her future groom,
Balanced blocks on a wooden floor
   inside a nursery room.

Where was I when a little cry
   came from her baby lips?
She, waving arms with teary eye,
   while I with hands on hips,
Boast of things I had done last night,
   with strings and snaps and zips.

Where was I when my wife first fell
   and scraped her tiny knees?
She, lifted up by her daddy, held
   until her sobbing eased,
While I, her groom, attempt to sail
   my kite on autumn's breeze

Where was I when my wife was young,
   my answered prayer to be?
She caught God's eye, the angels sung,
   while I prayed earnestly.
Find, Dear God, someone choice among
   Your daughters, just for me.

There was I when my wife's hand held
   her dad's arm for a while.
She, dressed in white and lace and veiled,
   while I with tears and smile,
Praised the Lord, as her dress trailed
   behind her down the aisle.

5. Proverbs 31:29 "Many daughters have done well, but you excel them all.'

### DAUGHTER TO DAD
### By Rachel Jean Reynolds

You come home from work sometimes
Tired and weary from all the problems you had to face.
Marines and recruits telling you all their troubles,
So many answers you put in their place.
Why do you do it? Because God called you to.
For you are a chaplain, your work you don't rue.

You use your time to listen and share, all of us know
how much you care.
Much time is put into your sermons in which you do prepare.
When you preach on Sunday mornings
you make us all aware of the things that went on long ago
and the things happening today.
You've shown many people the love of God, which is the only way.

Even after a long hard day,
And running with the recruits a mile,
You still have time to talk to me and show your tender smile.
I love you for being my dad and this is my advice to you:
Keep up the good work
and that friendly smile too.

6. Proverbs 27:11 "My son, be wise, and make my heart glad ..."

### THE MAN I SEE

She didn't see the tower of strength that weathers life's storms,

your toughness to stay the course when things get rough;
only unpleasant restraint.
She dismissed your tenderness as smothering,
too much affection rendered bothersome,
lacking latitude for living - her complaint.

The seasons and experiences of life make or mar
Our convictions, passion, prudence, and world view,
Fashioning our unique bent.
Sometimes spring rain is unhappily cursed
for spoiling picnic plans while some who thirst
receive the rain as blessing sent.

We, when scurrilously tossed away as unwanted,
might conclude the tosser rightly taunted our worth,
and question not the judgment given.
But, by betraying mutual trust and promise,
is the one who walks away who proved dishonest,
breaking sacred vow for some elusive heaven.

The man I see is unrelenting, tough and tender,
having roughness, boldness, mightiness, and splendor,
an intricate and intriguing spirit.
You, son, are the sweet rain of answered prayer,
a perfect gift to me from God with care,
I speak the truth in love, I hope you'll hear it.

7. Isaiah 44:3 "For I will pour water on him who is thirsty and floods on the dry ground; I will pour My Spirit on your descendants, and My blessing on your offspring ..."

## MY OFFSPRINGS' OFFSPRINGS

Breathless!
I'm not there now,
But I can see it and feel it.
My un-dipped brush cannot paint
What I more feel than see.

Perpetual movement!
It thrills me.
Like little birds in flight,
The more the commotion
The merrier it makes me.

Uncontaminated!
So fresh and funny.
My senses satiated,
Then and now again,
As I rethink upon that place.

Contentment!
Unlike any other.
My offspring's offspring,
To be wherever they are,
And long to see their face.

Amazement!
At how God blesses,
His undeserved gifts,
His promises received,
Bless Him O my soul!

8. Hebrews 12:1-2 "Therefore we also, since we are surrounded by so great a cloud of witnesses, let us lay aside every weight, and the sin which so easily ensnares us, and let us run with endurance the race that is set before us, looking unto Jesus, the author and finisher of our faith, who for the joy that was set before Him endured the cross, despising the shame and has sat down at the right hand of the throne of God."

## I'VE COME A LONG WAY

I've come a long way from where I first started.
No one can get here by being half-hearted.
Plaques cover my walls, books cover each shelf.
I'm tempted at times to brag on myself.

Yet I realize, I can't take full credit.
Please keep all your praise, I don't want to get it.
For I can recall a long list of faces,
Of people who helped in hundreds of cases:

A little old man, and two special preachers,
A seventh-grade friend, my Sunday School teachers,
Employers I've had, a bunch of professors,
Some neighbors, some kids, some dear intercessors.

I find I am much, much better for knowing,
These people who had a part in my growing.
It seems life each day gets better and better.
To all who have helped, I'll always be debtor.

But I cannot stop until I have said it.
I must give a few a whole lot of credit.

So, to my long list I must add four others:
My Jesus, my wife, my dad and my mother.

# FINAL WORDS

One thing I have learned from a lifetime of Christian ministry is that when the preacher or teacher says, "finally," it means nothing. He or she may have intended their next words to be their last, but don't count on it. Just look at the following scriptural examples:

2 Corinthians 13:11 "Finally, brethren, rejoice, be made complete, be comforted, be like-minded, live in peace; and the God of love and peace will be with you." Paul actually finished after this "finally" with only about thirty more words.

Ephesians 6:10 "Finally, be strong in the Lord and in the strength of His might." This was followed by fourteen verses.

Philippians 3:1 "Finally brethren, rejoice in the Lord." After this "finally" Paul wrote twenty more verses in that chapter followed by twenty-three verses in chapter four. These extra verses also included another "finally."

Philippians 4:8 "Finally, brethren, whatever is true, whatever is honorable, whatever is right, whatever is pure, whatever is lovely, whatever is of good repute, if there is any excellence and if anything worthy of praise, dwell on these things." This second "finally" in Philippians was followed by fifteen verses.

1 Thessalonians 4:1 "Finally then, brethren, we request and exhort you in the Lord Jesus, that as you received from us instruction as to how you ought to walk and please God just as you actually do walk, that you excel still more." As in the Philippians letter, this "finally" begins a chapter and is followed by a whole other chapter.

2 Thessalonians 3:1 "Finally, brethren, pray for us that the word of the Lord will spread rapidly and be glorified, just as it did also with you;…" While chapter three of 2 Thessalonians is the last chapter of this brief letter, it begins with the "finally' and is followed by seventeen more verses.

Finally, brothers and sister, this is the end. I am not going to expound any more or extol the joys of writing poetry. I am merely going to finish with these very few words. May God bless you and the ministry He has given to you. May you be faithful and true to our Lord and Savior and to the calling to which you have accepted from Him. My last words are the ten last words of our Holy Bible. "The grace of the Lord Jesus be with all. Amen."

# SCRIPTURE INDEX

| | | |
|---|---|---|
| Genesis 3:4-5 | Chapter Seven, #6 | The Serpent Lied |
| Genesis 12:1,4 | Chapter One, #2 | I Must When God Leads Me |
| Genesis 28:12 | Chapter Seven, #4 | Jacob's Dream |
| Genesis 50:24 | Chapter Seven, #1 | Moses |
| Exodus 16:1-2 | Chapter Three, #6 | Ev'ry Body Knows |
| Judges 6:36-38 | Chapter One, #6 | Give Me A Sign |
| 1 Samuel 3:9-10 | Chapter Five, #8 | Praying Some More |
| 1 Kings 19:11-12 | Chapter Seven, #2 | Ears Engaged |
| 2 Kings 20:9-10 | Chapter Seven, #5 | A Limerick On Hezekiah |
| Psalm 23:1-3 | Chapter Six, #5 | Green Pastures and Still Waters |
| Psalm 34:18 | Chapter Three, #3 | Relieve Their Pain |
| Psalm 37:4-7 | Chapter Three, #1 | My Heart's Desire |
| Psalm 63:1-8 | Chapter Five, #5 | A Desert Prayer |
| Psalm 51:10-12 | Chapter Five, #1 | Remaking My Heart |
| Psalm 73:21-24 | Chapter Five, #3 | I Hold Out My Hand |
| Psalm 91:10-11 | Chapter Two, #3 | When Trouble Hovers |
| Psalm 116:5-8 | Chapter Four, #5 | She Was Crying |
| Proverbs 3:5-8 | Chapter Eight, #7 | Separation or Divorce |
| Proverbs 4:5-8 | Chapter Two, #8 | My Library |
| Proverbs 14:26 | Chapter Ten, #2 | I Trust My Children Are Safe |

| | | |
|---|---|---|
| Proverbs 24:30-32 | Introduction | |
| Proverbs 27:11 | Chapter Ten, #6 | The Man I See |
| Proverbs 31:10 | Chapter Ten, #3 | One Wonderful Woman |
| Proverbs 31:29 | Chapter Ten, #5 | Daughter to Dad |
| Ecclesiastes 3:1-4 | Chapter Two, #2 | Work Is Never Done |
| Isaiah 44:3 | Chapter Ten, #7 | My Offspring's Offsprings |
| Isaiah 55:10-11 | Chapter Four, #6 | The Boy Didn't Listen |
| Daniel 6:10 | Chapter Five, #7 | My Evening Prayers |
| Daniel 6:23 | Chapter One, #1 | Stand for God |
| Matthew 6:6 | Chapter Five, #2 | I Need to Talk |
| Matthew 6:9 | Chapter Five, #6 | How to Pray |
| Matthew 6:9 | Chapter Nine, #1 | He Is My Father |
| Matthew 7:13,14 | Chapter Six, #7 | The Roman Road |
| Matthew 11:28-30 | Chapter Six, #3 | Come Unto Me |
| Matthew 11:29-30 | Chapter Two, #7 | Being Pastor Is Hard? |
| Matthew 19:14 | Chapter Five, #4 | The Sweetest Sound |
| Matthew 22:36-40 | Chapter Eight, intro | Loving People |
| Matthew 25:19-21 | Chapter Eight, #1 | To Serve You Well |
| Matthew 27:28-31 | Chapter Six, #1 | Ashamed |
| Mark 1:38 | Chapter Four, #1 | I Came to Preach |
| Mark 10:13-14 | Chapter Seven, #6 | All Are Precious |
| Luke 3:3-4 | Chapter Six, #4 | Going to Build a Highway |

| | | |
|---|---|---|
| Luke 18:18 | Chapter Six, #6 | If I Were a Rich Man |
| John 1:35-36 | Chapter Seven, #3 | Mary Had a Lamb |
| John 14:3 | Chapter Nine, #3 | Behold My Jesus |
| John 14:13 | Chapter Five, #6 | How to Pray |
| John 16:23-24 | Chapter Five, intro | Prayer |
| John 19:28-30 | Chapter Six, #2 | "It" Is a Word |
| Acts 5:40-42 | Chapter Four, intro | Preaching and Teaching |
| Acts 14:22-23 | Chapter Three, intro | Church |
| Acts 20:18-21 | Chapter Two, intro | The Minister's Work |
| Acts 21:5 | Chapter One, #7 | Leaving One Church for Another |
| Romans 5:13-14 | Chapter Nine, #6 | Conversation With Adam |
| Romans 8:38-39 | Chapter Eight, #2 | My Attitude of Others |
| Romans 10:9-10 | Chapter Six, intro | The Gospel of Jesus Christ |
| 1 Corinthians 2:4-5 | Chapter Four, #2 | You Preached It Very Well |
| 1 Corinthians 12:14 | Chapter Three, #8 | Feet Give Us Paws |
| 1 Corinthians 13:7, 8 | Chapter Eight, #6 | A Young Man |
| 2 Corinthians 5:1,4-7 | Chapter Nine, intro | Heaven |
| 2 Corinthians 6:3-5,9-10 | Chapter One, #3 | The Right Questions |
| 2 Corinthians 9:6-7 | Chapter Three, #4 | Give |
| 2 Corinthians 12:7 | Chapter Three, #7 | A Great Thorn |
| Galatians 1:11-12 | Chapter Four, #7 | Deliver the Sermon |

| Reference | Chapter | Title |
|---|---|---|
| Galatians 3:20 | Chapter Nine, #7 | What Death? |
| Ephesians 3:20 | Chapter Eight, #5 | Anything Can Happen |
| Ephesians 4:1-2 | Chapter Eight, #3 | Humility, Gentleness, and Patience |
| Ephesians 4:1-4 | Chapter One, intro | The Call to Christian Ministry |
| Ephesians 5:25 | Chapter Ten, #4 | My Wife Younger Than I |
| Philippians 1:23-24 | Chapter One, #4 | I Cannot Leave, I Love Them |
| Philippians 4:13 | Chapter Two, #6 | To Do All This |
| 1 Thessalonians 2:10-11 | Chapter Three, #2 | The Personality of a Church |
| 1 Thessalonians 4:13-14 | Chapter Nine, #4 | Give Me a Simple Funeral |
| 2 Thessalonians 1:2-3 | Chapter Eight, #4 | The Care Giver Treasure |
| 1 Timothy 3:4 | Chapter Ten, intro | The Christian Minister's Family |
| 2 Timothy 1:5 | Chapter Ten, #1 | My Grandson Norman |
| 2 Timothy 1:6-7 | Chapter Two, #4 | If God Gave Me Power |
| 2 Timothy 2:8-10 | Chapter Two, #1 | Working for God |
| 2 Timothy 3:16-17 | Chapter Four, #3 | God Inspired |
| 2 Timothy 4:2 | Chapter Four, #4 | What Would You Have Me to Say? |
| Hebrews 6:9-12 | Chapter One, #5 | I Will Not Resign |
| Hebrews 11:32-34 | Chapter Seven, intro | Bible Stories |
| Hebrews 12:1-2 | Chapter Ten, #8 | I've Come Along Way |
| 1 John 5:4-5 | Chapter Two, #5 | A Winning Attitude |

| | | |
|---|---|---|
| Revelation 19:5-7 | Chapter Nine, #5 | No One Knows |
| Revelation 22:3-4 | Chapter Nine, #2 | I Long for Heaven |

# ABOUT THE AUTHOR

Norman is a graduate of Samford University in Birmingham, Alabama; and Southwestern Baptist Theological Seminary in Fort Worth, Texas. He has served in various Christian Ministry roles in over 50 years including children and youth ministry during college and seminary, and afterward pastored two churches, thirteen years as active duty Navy Chaplain (which included time in Desert Storm), Associate Pastor of a large church with multi-ministries, chaplain of an assisted-living senior adult community, and chaplain at a rescue mission.

Norman's first book was published in 2007 titled *Women Pastors*, addressing the position Southern Baptists took in 2000 against allowing women to serve as senior pastors. After the publisher went out of business (not his fault), the book was re-published as *Female Pastors? The Case For Male Only*.

In 2012 Norman published an ebook titled: *True Humility, Finding Power and Joy in This Biblically Mandated Virtue*. This book was made available in hard copy in 2022. Late in November, 2021 Norman published *Commandments of Jesus* with WestBow Press. This book takes very seriously the words of Jesus in Matthew 28:20, "teaching them to observe all things that I have commanded you …". It sorts and consolidates Christ's teachings to provide a guide for assuring we are indeed teaching what He commanded.

Norman and his wife Connie have resided near Columbus, Georgia since 2004. He is still active in Christian ministry, serving as pastor of a small rural Baptist church.

www.ingramcontent.com/pod-product-compliance
Lightning Source LLC
Chambersburg PA
CBHW060334050426
42449CB00011B/2749